Praise for *Light Reading*

For many years, as the executive director of the United Religions Initiative, the Rev Charles Gibbs traveled the world, listening to everyone, lending a hand, and helping to wake the sleeping angels that hold the world up. He is a bridger who never shies from the truth and never gives up on our best selves. His writing now harvests the lessons and insights from years of service. There's medicine here.

— Mark Nepo, author of *The Endless Practice* and *The Book of Awakening*

These poems are little gems. Bright with truth and insight. Through them we bear witness to one man's pilgrimage through time, and watch him navigate a tender web of relationships. With his family, with Nature, with beauty and suffering, with his own soul, and with God. The result is a collection at once both personal and universal. And a gentle, yet insistent call, to remember what we are here for.

— Pavithra Mehta, author of *Infinite Vision: How Aravind Became the World's Greatest Business Case for Compassion*

Poetic expressions are the very core of cultural and national heritage, they create a universal language that we can understand and relate to. The poet may share with us his or her expressions of the beauty of the nature that surrounds us, what inspires the human heart, soothes our soul, and honors our humanity. The ordinary day becomes an everlasting experience, when the poet takes us to a distant time when love was in the air, spring was for celebration, friendship was the very core of human life, and the living nature was within our reach.

And *Poems from a Pilgrim Journey* embodies all that, letting us stay, even for a short while, to taste the sweet fragrance of a life's journey, with beautiful melodies and metaphors. What a magnificent journey, a journey that takes us away from the busy-ness of the everyday living and reminds us of the beauty of the human heart.

— Nahid Angha, Co-Founder, International Association of Sufism

These inspiring poems spoke profound as well as often delightful wisdom that left me freshly in touch with the deepest level of my own pilgrimage through life. They are truly "life giving" in the deepest meaning of that phrase. As such, I'm moved to re-read them again and again, as revealers of needed wisdom for the journey. Charles Gibbs is a true soul-friend for our more awake walk through life. He speaks from the depths of his own experience and spiritual awareness, grounded in a mature, mystical, world-inclusive sense of his faith.

—Tilden Edwards, Founder and Senior Fellow, Shalem Institute for Spiritual Formation

Heroes… their words and deeds, have long inspired the shape of culture and rightly so. Ours is a time in which the heroic remains relevant only if redefined to be inclusive, universal and spiritually mature. Charles Gibbs will be the first to deny he is a remarkable man, but in these pages he effectively redefines heroism by gently demonstrating that extraordinary intentions and acts of higher self and social meaningfulness reside in the co-ordinary fabric of who we each and all become as a human family, together. Together we must affirm, as does Charles in this book:

"I couldn't shake the feeling that something in the depth of my being, something at the heart of creation, was calling me into deeper relationship with it and calling me to lead a moral and ethical life of service to the world."

—Barbara Fields, Executive Director, Association for Global New Thought, Co-founder & Director, Gandhi King Season for Nonviolence

Light Reading

Light Reading

– Poems From a Pilgrim Journey –

Charles P Gibbs

ISBN: 1515195600
ISBN 13: 9781515195603
Library of Congress Control Number: 2015912074
CreateSpace Independent Publishing Platform
North Charleston, South Carolina

For my family
with endless love and gratitude

We sleep for this --
we dream
we wake
in the deep night's
stippled dark
to find ourselves
in that quiet crystal place
where poems are born.

Contents

Preface

Our birth is but a sleep and a forgetting
The Soul that rises with us, our life's Star,
    Hath had elsewhere its setting,
    And cometh from afar:
    Not in entire forgetfulness,
    And not in utter nakedness,
But trailing clouds of glory do we come
    From God, who is our home...
            William Wordsworth

My entire life has been a pilgrimage of remembrance. When I was a young boy growing up in Socorro, New Mexico, I once bolted after my mother as she went forward to receive communion, calling, I want to get drunk, too. My mother's memory is that I actually said, I want some beer, too. In either case, the message is clear to me – from my earliest days, in ways deeper than intellectual understanding, I have been drawn into what our Sufi sisters and brothers call divine intoxication.

I don't know why that call has been so relentless and yet it has. Even when I ran away from the Church and tried to run away from an understanding of God I'd outgrown, it turned out that I was still on the same pilgrimage of remembrance. It has been a pilgrimage of dying to the myriad false selves that keep us forgetful in this life and being reborn into an ever-deeper understanding of our true self, which is a reflection of the One that is our home – the source and power of love, which I believe is ultimately sovereign.

The world's religions, spiritual and indigenous traditions refer to the One by myriad different names and by no name at all, like so many fingers pointing at the moon, to borrow an insight from the Buddha. Those differences deserve to be respected; and yet I believe that they don't matter ultimately. The One is the One no matter what name we use.

Mine has been a pilgrimage of ecstatic joy and deep belonging. Of alienation and profound despair as I felt completely lost in the fog of forgetting. Of the healing light of remembering. Of deep inner reflection and passionate, compassionate service in this wondrous and wounded world.

I don't believe we reach the end of this pilgrim journey in our lifetime on Earth. I don't believe we ever transcend the cycle of death and rebirth. But I do believe, as we allow ourselves to surrender completely to the One, that death and rebirth become indistinguishable from each other, at the same time that they will always be different.

The poems in this volume are drawn from nearly four decades of my pilgrim's journey. Though the general sweep is from earlier poems to current ones, from being more lost to feeling more found, older and more recent poems are intermixed throughout. I believe these poems reflect truth about my experience as a pilgrim. If, occasionally, I have strayed from factual accuracy in a poem based on my life experience, it has been in my effort to capture more concisely and perhaps symbolically what to me was the deep truth of an event or a relationship.

I pray these poems speak to you in ways that invite, support and challenge you on your journey of remembrance, your journey into your heart, which is the heart of the One.

Voice of Sophia
for Marcus

The voice of Sophia, the voice of God's Wisdom,
Insistently calls us to come journey on,
To pack few belongings, to trust in her guidance,
To set out in darkness, to come journey on --

The voice of Sophia calls us out of bondage,
Held captive by Pharaoh and fearful of dawn.
She leads us in darkness, through death to deliverance,
Then into the wilderness, come journey on --

The voice of Sophia, in cloud and in fire,
Inspires our courage and guides us toward dawn,
Obscured by resistance. Then God's transformation:
Light shines in the wilderness, come journey on --

O voice of Sophia be spoken within us.
Enlighten our struggle from darkness to dawn.
Enliven the joy that is trembling within us,
Deep joy at your calling to come journey on --

Where Light Awaits

Maps are a distraction
Surrender –
your heart has eyes to guide you
into the dark wilderness
where light awaits.

So Long

It is night now.
The Jack Daniels is almost gone,
and so am I.

A rotten pair of sneakers,
thrown away.
Leaky windows never got fixed,
I'm leaving my pots behind.
More ants in the frying pan,
you can have the Black Flag.
Faded dirty rug,
I'll leave the carpet sweeper;
there's an energy crisis, you know.

The plastics factory goes on
buzzing like a mosquito.
World map off the wall,
into my suitcase.
Packing almost finished,
and so am I.

It is night now,
night into morning.
And so am I.

Water Awaits

Perhaps you are lost
in the desert where
no plants seem to grow.
Appreciate the arid beauty.
Move onward.
Water awaits.

Goodness Inside

Are you sometimes so far
from the person you want to be?
Why not take one step
today to draw nearer
to the goodness inside?

Holy

How long since I sat
comfortable in a church pew?
It's what they want
when they pass the plate:
to take you to the altar all *mea culpa*;
to bring you back, changed.

So long since I sat comfortable,
still, there is in me a yearning,
when my dog nudges with her nose,
paws at my arm, and
with her I moan:
I want.

Who is there to pat me?
To come home and let me in?
Whose bed can I sleep by
when I need to rest?
And why, goddamnit, so long
since I sat comfortable

Why Wait Your Whole Life

Why wait your whole life
for an unambiguous message
from on high?

There are a million universes
in each beating of your heart.

Be still.
Listen.
Dissolve.

When you return
you will be light,
guided into the heart
of surrender and service.

Bringing Joy

Imagine the joy
your inner beauty
blossoming outward
can bring to someone
unknown and on the edge.

Secret Inside

There's a secret inside
that I guess at mostly, maybe glimpse:
it's like the difference between
the thin-walled box room
of this Albuquerque motel,
and the Rio Grande rushing,
springtime high and fast,
such a short drive away.

Tremble for me once,
open once and let me inside.
I pray this late at night
when the springtime is gone,
the Rio Grande low and slow;
when the house is asleep
and the only light anywhere
is blinding.

The Journey Awaits

Close the door to your room.
Sit in stillness, waiting
by the newly open window.
Outside, the air is fresh.
The journey awaits.

New Moon Night

I yawn, my stomach growls,
the light turned out,
but I cannot sleep.
The dog in me wants to be let out.

Silent Night

Leaving the farm house,
walking the windy pastures,
dogs and stars my companions and guardians,
yet, windblown and cold,
I walk alone, seeking you;
knowing if I found you
I would be afraid.

I lie tense in expectation,
face-up to the stars,
the dogs keeping watch,
one at my head, one at my feet.
The wind blows cold up my jacket.
I know you might come.
Yet, I fear
the sound of footsteps.

What is it I seek
at night in the starry fields,
so intently, so hopefully,
and yet so full of fear?

Deep inside, do I refuse
to accept that I must die
to be reborn?
Do I lack the faith in new life
that quiets the fear of dying?

Alone, at night
in the silvery fields, whistling,
whispering wind blowing cold
on my ears and nose, blowing
the full moon into the sky,
I know this is where to find you.

Yet, I stand
and leave.

Beginning of Beauty

Why not risk breaking
open, trusting
that brokenness is
the beginning of beauty
waiting to blossom.

October Monkshood

Open for me flower.
I will keep you company
through the coming winter kill.

Open for me flower.
The world is closing down,
and I need to grow.

Open for me flower.

Over My Head

I

New-fallen leaves pad the path
we walk beside the Concord River.
Their rustling stirs an urge
to spring far ahead, but
I hold back – helping my
grandmother, hobbled by her
arthritic legs; steering my grandfather,
whose sight dims each day.

We talk of my uncle, killed
as a child, and of my father,
so remote. "I lived through that
dying," my grandmother says.
"They both seemed dead to me."

My grandfather asks the time.
The ball game's starting soon.
"He has to watch on TV since
he's gone deaf," she says.
"That's all that's left. And walking,
when his phlebitis isn't too bad."

He whistles a soft tune, smiles, says
she thinks it's worse than it is.
"As long as I go first," she says.
"I'm afraid to be left alone,
afraid of falling to pieces
with your father so far away."
My grandfather strokes her
trembling hand: "It's all right,
babe. The game isn't over yet."

II

Grandpa, you were a young
day by the radio rooting for
the Red Sox. You liked that best.

No more.
Age stole your sound.
Then it stole your sight.
You could scarcely see to walk.
Then, when it took your leg,
shut you in, you overcame
that last embarrassment,
died wet in your chair.

I won't remember you that way.

III

I wheel my grandmother
to twin tombstones. She
blows kisses to her husband
and her son. Rolling beside
the river, she aches to mother
her other son at last, then
cries aloud from her arthritic
love, and is silent.

IV

Over my head in the dark
beside the Concord River,
a meteor slides down the sky,
then dies in a burst of light –
calls to mind our soon-to-be-born
son whose new life might shine
light for my hiding father, for
my grandmother in her mourning,
the redemption of a memory:

"It's all right, babe.
The game isn't over yet."

Awaken

Our deeper, truer self
lies dormant, expectant,
waiting for us to awaken
to its insistent urging –
Break through the husk.
Blossom.

To Debbie

At school, they joked
with you: morning sickness,
just like Julie, and
that nagging tiredness
won't go away
but grows.

I'm pregnant, they think,
you told me. You had
an appointment to see
the nurse practitioner.
It was the doctor's day off.
You explained so well,
it really can't be, but
I don't know what else, I'm
just not getting over it.

Four days later,
neither am I –
not that you are,
but that you aren't.

When you first
used that word,
for yourself,
for us, I knew
these many years of fearing
the real mystery of love
had ended. And I
wanted to hear from you
I love that we are
going to have a baby.

You Lie With A Smile

You lie with a smile above
this baby growing in you.
I hurry off my robe,
move the jealous cat from
the warmth by your belly.
I need to be near that roundness.

Dear Dad,

The mail in Venezuela is so poor,
I hope this gets to you.
At last, it is spring.
Our garden is in.
It's winter there, I suppose.
We were always that way,
even together.

It isn't as much your
younger brother's early
death that pains me,
as how young you were, left
alive and needing her love –
a brittle leaf pressed between
the pages of a book.

You grew without her
noticing she raised
a son with love withered and dry
like a leaf from a dying tree.

The distance between us
doesn't pain me as much
as trying to reach you
when all the help I have
is the smell of burning leaves
and so much smoke in my eyes.

I wish you could be here
when our garden's in bloom.
You always visit in the winter,
welcome as the first snow, but
nothing grows in the frozen ground.
The cut flowers you bring
linger a few days, then,
like you, they are gone.
I wish we could be together
to share our garden's first fruit.

Beyond Wounds

If you look deeper
beyond wounds,
wounded, wounding –
you discover, one day
all scars dissolve –
in the meantime,
how will you live?

Flying on One Leg

The early sun a red disc hung
in the hazy Punjabi sky as
I walk ahead of the day's heat.

On the lightly dewed grass,
a strange bird hops slightly
lopsided on its one thin leg.

Was it I wonder born this way
like the man outside the gurudwara
with deformed feet facing backwards?

Or was it the victim of an attack
or an accident like so many
of the world's vulnerable poor?

The answer, for the bird, is less
important than, having only one
leg, still being able to fly.

Empty

The journey demands preparation.
Empty your pockets;
then empty them again.
You will be surprised
by riches along the way.

Birthing

My son is not quite four,
but he's bigger than many
good-sized six-year-olds.
He eats constantly,
loves to laugh,
to hear his friend, Fred Rogers,
say how special he is,
to take him to the
Neighborhood of Make-believe.

In my imagination
I often live through my son's death,
die through his death,
because I can't make believe
living through it.

Today he threw two new pieces
of string cheese into the garbage.
Like an inaccurate expert,
he said, "See,
these are hard."

How can I tell him --
all over the world
children are starving;
parents are dying through
what I can't even make believe?

Is the aching in my stomach
something to be ignored?
Or, I wonder, the labor pain
of Christ being born within me?
And what does it ask of me?

If there is an answer,
it is in the stillness
before my son's first heartbeat,
after the last heartbeat
of a starving infant.
It is in the yearning:
that brings us into life;
that, in life, draws us
ever closer to the divine risk --
that in death is eternal birth.

Outside of that death,
that risk, that birth,
I stand aching,
yearning, bewildered, in love;
while starving babies die,
and my son chews soft cheese.

Inner Eye

Even in the darkness
you can journey onward.
Turn your eyes inward.
Even on an overcast night
there are stars to guide you.

Step Out

You can't hold back spring.
Step out the door.
You might discover your life
is bursting with fresh blossoms.

Minnesota Spring

In the kitchen,
clean from a swim in the lake,
Pete licks his paws dry, and
whines to go out in the mud.

Sorrow to Joy

If you are still enough
you can hear cries
of joy and sorrow.
Reach out your hand.
Help someone move
from sorrow to joy.

Undying

I

Years ago, seeking rest in my fearful confusion,
I nightly walked out under the Oklahoma sky,
lay down in the rolling earth's flowering alfalfa,
and, losing all sense of myself,
rolled with it, boundaries between
earth, stars, and me,
my fears and confusion
all dissolved.

One night, on the edge in the freshly mown field,
earth wind-swept, clouds scudding lowly across the sky,
I was seized by the sense unbidden
that if I raised my eyes I would find
Jesus Christ striding across the pasture to me.
I froze -- afraid to remain,
unable to rise.

II

Now at night, I lie open to the sky,
or what passes for the sky in this closed-in apartment,
on my back, arms outstretched,
hoping to ease away the day's tensions
caught like knots around my neck and shoulders,
to relax into nothing and to find myself there·
at ease, at one, at rest, at peace;
all the edges gone -- a part of the presence of God,

But on this night I am disturbed,
jerked prematurely from my emptying
by the sound of my three-year-old son
brushing his pajamed feet against
the insubstantial partition of his room.
His sleep is fitful, like my spirit.
I feel drawn to him, tied to him,
as often I was when, newborn,
he slept so effortlessly, so silently
that his life seemed to leave his body
and inhabit some invisible life
that filled me with the fear of death.

I stood achingly long,
leaning over his crib,
afraid to touch, to rouse,
to recall him to life.
Then, unbidden, a tiny pink finger
unfolded from his hand
toward me:
a touch through space,
the spark of life.

III

Tonight, with unbidden suddenness,
the image of my son's death swallows me.
I dissolve in a lifeless silence
that robs me of small arms around my neck,
of a hand grasping just one finger as we walk together.
What use now for my finger?
For my neck?
For me?

This is like an aching for God,
but worse, because God never hugged me goodnight,
or listened as I read stories,
or helped with the laundry, or the shopping,
or shared my glory at the early rising moon,
the early setting sun.
God never needed me as my son does,
and I wonder if I ever need God as I do my son?

IV

Out of this empty unbidden pain,
uneased even by the sure knowledge
that my son lies living a few feet away,
issues another unbidden vision:

an old man, beyond the age of hope,
but blessed by a son;
standing, as I imagine, under the open sky,
his eyes lifted as mine are,
open and aching for a presence.
To him, unbidden, comes a voice,
the fearful presence of God:

"Abraham!"
And not knowing what to answer:
"Here I am."

"Take your son, your only son,
Isaac, whom you love,
and bind him and slay him
and burn his lifeless body,
that I may know you love me."

For Abraham, I want to answer:
Then who will love me?

V

This isn't what I expected to find
lying open to God --
my tears at the death of a son still alive;
Abraham's faith at the life of a son he must kill.
What have I been looking for all these years of nights?
What have I found that I more readily
give Abraham my fear
than take his faith:

the faith to rise,
to begin the fearful journey
to the wounding, healing, undying
love of God.

Waking

How can we sleep,
as if not knowing,
when our souls are
drawn to the moment
the sun bursts forth?

Simply Cease

Each of us is
a contained expression
of the infinite,
of the ultimate.

Strive for at least
an instantto slip
loose the container
and simply
cease to be.

Baptism

When he waded into Jordan's swift water
where John had cleansed so many,
did he know what would happen?

Did he know that when he moved from the shore,
saw the gray green water swirl ever higher up his legs,
until it rose almost to his heart;

did he know when John cradled his head
in an instant of deadly tenderness
and then plunged him into oblivion;

that he would be dead before he rose,
and arising would feel a new weight,
as light as a dove on his shoulder,
as heavy as all human pain,
as biting as the sharpest treachery in love;

did he know
and still
say yes?

Each of Us Will Die One Day

Each of us will die one day –
it doesn't matter.
More important is to practice living.

Still all that does not serve
our truest becoming.
Listen to the music of the universe
inviting us to begin
the dance that is ours alone.

The Beloved has been waiting
from before time
for our first step
for our next step.

No matter our age,
our life is new in this moment –
Let us dance.

Wise Guides

You don't need anyone's permission
to be who you truly are
but you do need wise guides.
They linger just beyond
the edge of your seeing,
awaiting only your invitation.

Aurora
...for learning together

Small seeds, like cumin with a thorn,
stick to my poncho in clusters
caught from the northern lights.
As I sit at my campsite
picking them from the wool,
all around me tents
are walking into cars.

Soon the campground will be empty.
Soon the grass will bounce back.
There's no hurry with these seeds,
I'll see to them once I'm home.

Are You Thirsty?

The water of life
from the deepest well
slakes any thirst.
Why not simply surrender
and dive in?

Forever

This late January day
I will live forever—
the sky is ocean blue
and these naked trees
float like strange seaweed
in the golden dusk.

Some say as we were swept
from the teeming seas eons
ago onto waiting sand we
heard in the gently crashing waves
the Divine Mother urging us to emerge
knowing we would never
be truly at home on dry land.

So we await our return drawn by
the insistent pull of tidal time and
the intuition that we will never die.

Again, the Snow

Again, the snow --
even the weighted branches
swaying against the muted sky
share in this deep stillness.

Such A Vast Opening

Such a vast opening from here
to the horizon -- sky rising endlessly,
waves gliding on the face of the unfathomable
deep, beneath a small wooden boat
where a solitary soul fishes for life.

Ashore men huddle at the sea's edge
studying some curiosity in the swirling sand
until a wave washes it away and they idle
up the beach seeking a new sight,
then another, then another, as if the deepest
secrets are to be glimpsed ashore.

I stand uneasily in the sand -- drawn
by the far horizon and the high sky
to a small boat riding the swells
as a solitary soul lowers his net deeper
and deeper into the source of life.

I Slip Loose the Nets

I slip loose the nets
I have entangled myself in
and sliding into the open water
cast my lot with mystics and poets

Oh, Pilgrim

Oh, pilgrim,
in your forgetful
striving to surrender,
pause a moment
to remember:

It is beyond our control —

and, yet, unless we forget
the light that beckons
we are compelled to *seek* —
breath by breath,
until we breathe no more.

It is beyond our control —

and, yet, if we remember
seeking begins with surrender and
still our stumbling in the deep dark
long enough to listen to the light,
we will lose our fear
that we are lost or alone.

It is beyond our control —

and, yet, if in surrender we
trust the journey, always
beginning and never ending,
and wise guides with us always,
we will abide endlessly
in the joyous light of
death and rebirth.

Oh, pilgrim, the moments

of our lives are too fleeting
to waste in dark forgetfulness.
The light beckons,
journey on –
remember, surrender;
embrace death, discover life.

Ash Wednesday

This cross of ashes
on our foreheads
calls us to remember
we come from star dust
and are made to shine.

The Call of This Moment

The call of this moment
and of all moments
is to seek the light
and to face the darkness
within and without
with unflinching honesty
and unswerving devotion
to journey at least a little each day
toward enlightenment –
living in love,
fearless, joyous and free –
in service
to this glorious and wounded world.

Why Hesitate?

Imagine for a moment
we have the power
to remake the world
in light.

Your gift, your
service is exactly
what is lacking.

Why hesitate?

Being Truly Alive

Sorrow is the suspended moment
before dawn's first light
and death no more
than the infinitesimal pause
between the in-breath and the out.

Who would stop breathing
to avoid death
or flee back into the night
to avoid sorrow?

To awaken we must
embrace sorrow and death –
all is tomb, all is womb;
so enter with gladness
the suspended moment
before dawn's first light,
embrace for all eternity
the endlessly infinitesimal pause
between the in-breath and the out.

Let all distraction drop away;
listen deeply – be undefended.
The Beloved beckons.
With each breath, die and be reborn
into the endless and unexpected
mystery of being truly alive.

Goodness Awaits

Yes, the day's news
brings plenty to worry about.
The sky is cloudy.
Storms abound.
Still, the choice is ours –
goodness awaits.

Never Alone

Whether your hand reaches
out in need or to offer aid
another hand awaits.
You are never alone.

New Jaipalguri Train Station

She was so slight beneath her sari –
the deep mysteries of the universe
shone in her eyes and the ravages
of poverty hacked in her cough
and the baby nestled against her
barely-there breast exhaled
a low, weary, wanting murmur.

What was I to do –
besides gaze long into her eyes
and silently bless her and her infant?

Before her had come an older woman
jabbing the gauze-swathed stump
of what had once been an arm
in my face for emphasis
while her remaining hand first
mimed scooping food into her mouth
and then reached out to me for money,
staring all the while with her fathomless eyes.
I'm ashamed to acknowledge that
I wondered if in this crazy cruel world
her arm had been purposefully amputated
to make her a more compelling beggar.

What was I to do –
besides gaze long into her eyes
and silently bless the humanity
hidden beneath her deformity ?

As we stood eyes locked
a slightly stooped man intruded with
an almost perfunctory plea for alms
and though he moved on in search of
a more promising target
I could imagine a vast ocean
of pleading eyes and jabbing stumps
and outstretched hands
and infants too young to know
the sentence they received
before they were born
and the indifference, greed
and hardened hearts
that dehumanize and exploit.

With wave after wave crashing
over me what was I to do
besides gaze long into all their eyes
knowing they laid on me a claim
I would carry long after I climbed
into a taxi and drove away
wondering if these people
with their haunted, haunting eyes
were more human to me than I to them,
and wondering what I would do.

Enough to Share

As you dig deep
to prepare the soil
ponder what you will
plant in your garden.
Will there be enough
to share?

Opening Invisible Doors

Each day so many new walls
looming tall and topped
with concertina wire.

Let us journey together,
opening invisible doors
to let in the light.

Words of Love From The Edge of Despair

The innocent dead
don't care
how noble or despicable
the motives of those
who killed them.

The innocent dead
don't care whether they were killed
by an American drone attack
or a Taliban mortar
or an Israeli bomb
or a Palestinian rocket
or a bullet from the rifle
of a government or a rebel soldier –

or die of starvation
or of preventable illness

while the world goes mad
with spending on armaments –
and, yes, the United States
leads the world by far
in this spending –
that will never
ultimately make the world safer.

Mahatma Gandhi said,
An eye for an eye and
the whole world will be blind.

John Donne wrote –
Any one's death diminishes me
for I am involved in humankind.

We are blinded.
Our humanity is diminished.

And all the arguments about
who is right and who is wrong
will not bring back the dead,
or save the lives of those,
so many women and children
who are innocently in the way
of the next bomb or bullet,
or feed a hungry person
or cure a preventable disease
or build a better future.

So what are we,
the living, to do,
blinded and diminished
as we are?

We can raise our voices
against this madness.
We can rededicate ourselves
to weaving the fabric of a new
community of compassionate action
a seamless garment of love and justice
for all our Earth community.

We can, but will we?
Ask the innocent dead
whose cries rise like smoke
into the weeping skies.

Soften

Even the frozen soil
of your guarded heart
can soften in spring's warming.

Turn toward
the strengthening sun.

Tributaries of Good

Another bombing in Karachi.

How does evil flow
so fiercely through our world --
a river we cannot dam?

So, feed the tributaries of good.

Better to Burn

Better to burn 1,000 holy books
than to deface creation
or harm one child of God.

Better still, honor holy books –
celebrate creation; embrace
God's diverse children.

These Beautiful Faces
for all the Michael Browns

These beautiful faces – black
brown, yellow, red, white
shining with joyous
brightness of inner light.

Thank you, Loving Light – guide
us to cherish this great gift.

On This Day of Days

On this day of days,
my soul beholds arrays
of rising light shining
through the empty tomb
and sings with joy.

The Way Back, The Path Forward

Once we knew and forgot.

For millennia we have labored
to find our way; yet now we accelerate
in the slow stream of stars
drawn relentlessly toward extinction.

Is now even the sun our enemy –
we descendants of Icarus,
patron saint of those whose cleverness
so far outstrips their wisdom

that we become a horde of locusts
exhausting Earth's abundance,
leaving no place even to hibernate
until Earth heals herself.

Some say we're not to blame;
others that it's too late.
So we continue clear-cutting and
contemplate ever-higher sea walls.

The cosmos is infinitely patient
and even the sun will one day die –
species survival isn't the issue, but
what we will leave behind should

haunt and inspire us no longer to rely on
the seductive wings of wanting and war
and in urgent times embrace Earth, seek
the light and serve the long walk to wisdom,

alert along the way for wise guides
and unlikely allies on this long,
urgent journey forward and back
into the great circle of light

that once we knew and may know again.

Time To Be Still

Time to be still,
to listen deeply, to look inwardly –
death is the passage;
new life the reward.
Will you journey on?

The Frozen Earth

The frozen earth
rock hard underfoot
on my moonlight walk
through these barren woods
soon to be filled
with fragrant blossoms.

Will The Last Human

Will the last human
alive on Earth
remember to say,
"Thank you.
We're sorry."

And will we
wait until then
to awaken?

9/11

As an American I am
compelled to ask, why,
in the aftermath of 9/11
violation and death, my nation
chose the path of more
violation and death when
through the blaze of shared
global grief a path of light
lay open before us?

Transformation

Hatred and tyranny
are born in malformed
hearts and minds.
True revolution begins
in transforming the malformed –
becoming truly human.

Humanity's Epitaph

Select our epitaph –

Unable to share
Earth's boundless
abundance.

Or...

Awakening at the edge,
grew wings of humility
compassion and mercy.

Imagination's Wings

The land of cataclysm and doom!
Don't die there. Dare
to soar on imagination's wings
into the dawn of new creation.

The migration begins!

Hiroshima

Closing my eyes
I see the dome raked
naked against a cloudless sky,

a crown of devastation
atop ruined walls of brick and rubble
where once a building stood,

where once a city stood;
where a city stands still
an atomic phoenix.

Symphony of Peace Prayers
for Masahisa Goi

This symphony of peace prayers
rising from Earth's aching heart
sounds notes so deep, so high, so pure
they pierce the world ego, opening

a way to the One, the Source of all
wisdom – empty and overflowing
sound and silence abiding in the moving
stillness of eternal becoming:

Guide us, we pray, away from folly
far from shore into open waters
where cleansed and renewed we flow
forth as the limitless light of peace.

Turning for the Ethiopian Millennium *for Mussie*

Let these waves of the
Arabian Sea wash over us,
deep, gentle, irresistible,
as west across its vast expanse
the thousand years turn
in the cradle of humanity
beckoning us to be born anew.

Let the waves wash over us,
draw us from dry sand
into deep water
toward a far horizon
to a new shore
waiting to welcome us home.

Let the waves wash over us
and over us and over us
until we are as pure as infants
emerging from deep waters
at the edge of new life.

Morning Terrace in Kottarakkara

Now the sun seeps through the clouds
the breeze rustles the leaves –
mimosa, banana, papaya and coconut palm,
freeing last night's rain – liquid light
suspended, then falling,
as all eventually falls.

Birds whose names I don't know
sings songs as old as memory,
as fresh as this new day;
and children walk,
by ones and twos,
through this shimmering song of life
as naturally as the singing birds
or the falling drops of light.

I sit on the terrace, recalling
songs beyond memory and rising light.

Stillness Settles Over Lake Dunmore

As I sit on the cabin deck at sunset
stillness settles over Lake Dunmore –
on the sloping hillside below oaks and
pines aglow in the late afternoon sun;

lost in the lake's shimmering gold
the soulful song of a loon searching
for its mate. Oh, this lovely
wounded world is filled with light.

I am being drawn out of my body
into the growing, glowing stillness.
Is this the way it will be,
I wonder, just before I die?

Where Music Comes From
for Gwhyneth Chen

I'm not sure where music comes from
but I know you are.
I've seen you settle yourself
onto a piano bench –
deeply-rooted as a mountain
rising into thin air – then pausing,
flow over the keys like a willow
caressing the surface of a stream,
the music of the universe yearning
to be drawn out of the piano,
out of your being,
out of thin air…

…and filling the thin air –
the rush of stream over rocks
the whip of wind through cascading willows
the brightness of afternoon sun in summer
the warmth of baking earth
the silent sound of golden poppies
invisibly unfurling as day shines night away.

They call it playing and I suppose it is
playing, as the Buddha played
once he had awakened
and saw so deeply
beyond the veil of illusion
into the heart of being.

You have journeyed there, I imagine,
because I have no other way
to comprehend your playing
except to believe it is born
anew in each instant
in that mysterious universe
where music comes from
inside your heart.

The Mountain Seat
for Fu

Oh, Fu, you seemed so frail,
so weighed down, as you climbed
the mountain – head shaven,
hand encircling the substantial staff
that seemed more burden than support.

Step by slow, winding step,
the spirit of selfless service,
you rose above the sangha –
a plain peopled with unbounded
gratitude, respect and love.

As you reached the peak,
beheld the shining sea of love below,
you shone like an ancient sage.

A smile like the rising sun
lit your already-luminous face
with a new light of wonder,
of confidence, of joy.

In that moment, you wore
your robes so well –
a Buddhist Moses, radiant
with the light of seeing
the Ultimate face-to-face.

The sun stood still
for a timeless flow
of heart and mind,
of wit and wisdom,
of tears and laughter.

Then the sun moved again
and you descended – staff
no longer a burden of
strange responsibility and authority
but an extension of your Self.

Transformed, you reentered
the sangha – radiant with a light
kindled long before you were born,
a new light that through time and tears,
through love and fears will shine
ever brighter and brighter
in selfless service.

Wild Geese
for Master Hui Liu

We were born this way –
flying featherless,
unfettered flow of qi,
as easy as breathing;
until, awakening
to this world,
our true home
became a distant dream.

The high haunting call,
the graceful flight
of the wild geese,
awaken memories
too long earth bound.

Like each new day,
we are reborn –
losing our self
in focused gracefulness,
taking wing
on dawn's gentle breeze,
we rise like wild geese,
like liquid light of qi,
and turning homeward
embrace our essence.

The high haunting call,
the graceful flight –
no longer earth bound,
we become one
with the wild geese,
rising endlessly
on the invisible
streams of life.

Easter

Clouds forecast…

Still the sun dances
on the pink blossoms
of the flowering plum.

To Be Still Enough

Perched on the high Himalayan
slopes of cloud-shrouded Darjeeling,
this gracious old hotel, built
in 1887 as the summer residence
of the Maharaja of Cooch Behar,
with its wide-plank wood floors
and musty overstuffed chairs
sitting beside the glowing coal fire,
calls unexpectedly to mind
a remote place and time –
8,000 miles and decades away
in Litchfield, Connecticut
where my grandmother lived.

Peaceful House – built the year
before the American Revolution,
of white clapboard, with green shutters,
wood plank floors and overstuffed
chairs sitting beside a crackling wood fire;
dooryard maples flanked the front walk
and a grassy backyard tumbled
down through the woods to where
the Goshen River wound its way
to a beaver pond and spilling
over the log dam flowed
downward toward the sea.

I have lived several lifetimes
since I last wandered through
those woods and along the river,
yet I seem to remember
that once I succeeded
in being still enough
for long enough to
glimpse a beaver.

That may have happened
only in my imagination, though,
from the distance of four decades,
I wonder whether imagining
isn't as good as actually having seen –
I've forgotten so much of my life
and the sense of wonder
and gratitude is equally
rich a blessing either way.

I know there's a great deal
for which I still must make amends –
none of us passes harmlessly
through this life, no matter
how pure our intentions –
which is why sitting high
on the Himalayan slopes I'm so grateful
to be reminded of Peaceful House
and of Grandma. She loved me
so easily, so openly,
so unconditionally, so lightly
that when I was with her I
only ever wanted to be better.

Even now, as I sit in distant
Darjeeling decades after her death
and hear the haunting call to prayer
of a muezzin emerge from the cloud-shrouded
minaret of a nearby mosque
and imagine her beside me,
I want to be better.

I've only ever wanted my life
to be a prayer (except, of course,
for when I've forgotten,
which, to be honest,
has been far too often).
I'm at an age where
what matters most to me is
to make each breath a prayer,
the event of a lifetime filled
with gratitude, wonder,
commitment, surrender.

They say if the clouds clear
in Darjeeling you can see
rising into the breathless sky
the snow-capped heights of
Kangchenjunga – the Five Treasures of Snow.
But the clouds don't clear
and sitting in the glow of a coal fire
I have only faded photographs
and my imagination.

Litchfield, Darjeeling or anywhere else,
whether I actually saw a beaver or not,
whether the clouds burn away or not,
whether a grandmother long passed away
can be present in a different world and time
or not, the mystery is there in each moment
if only we will be still enough
for long enough to be filled with wonder
and endlessly grateful.

Invite Gratitude

How many times today
or in your whole life
have you said, Thank you?
Why not invite gratitude
to transform your life.

Gratitude Enough

Outside my study window
leaves again turn red
and soon will fall.
No regret, yet I wonder,
is my gratitude enough for
what has been and what lies ahead?

Assembling Cribs

In a lifetime so long ago it seems
more myth than history I sat,
awaiting the birth of our
soon-to-be first-born,
on the yellow linoleum floor
of our soon-to-be nursery
and assembled a crib –

light hardwood, birch or ash
like Minnesota's northern forests,
with shining steel fittings
to hold the screws in place,
a plastic teething sleeve atop the
side drop-rails and on the ends
bright red and blue and yellow
spinning balls–
to make it happy.

As I remember I sat
or knelt all alone in a mass
of cardboard and packing paper,
the hardware sorted, the directions
and tools at hand, and made
my way through assembly,
step by step and sometimes
as in life discovering I'd
misread the signals
and had to retrace my steps.

Still, the moment came when the crib
was complete and the proud papa-to-be
stood satisfied that I had contributed
to the next step of the great adventure
growing large in my wife's stomach.

Thirty years later, kneeling –
with stiffer knees and graying hair
but no less a sense of wonder –
on a carpeted floor of a Houston
bedroom with three dark, deep blue walls,
and Ben, our first-born, surrounded
by cardboard and plastic bags –
dark wood and no drop-rails;
hardware, tools, instructions
to assemble not one but twin cribs
as this new papa-to-be prepares
to step into parenthood.

I'm Awake
for Abby and Henry

One moment absolute stillness
then a slight rustle of blanket
the subtle parting of tiny lips
a twitch of tiny feet
an arm shifts slightly.

Then in an instant
arms waving wildly
feet flailing
siren-screams erupting.

Later they will learn to say
I'm awake.
For now, this will have to do.

Blessing for a New Tomorrow

Written for the International Day of Peace, 21 September 2005 and read by those gathered at the Isaiah Wall across 1ˢᵗ Avenue from the United Nations to plant a grape vine to bear the fruit of peace, justice and healing for all.

We gather here today to plant a new tomorrow,
fulfilling the prophet's ancient vision –
swords into ploughshares, spears into pruning hooks,
and, yes, land mines into grape vines.

We gather here today to plant a new tomorrow
whose harvest will be not the grapes of wrath
but the fruit of peace, justice and healing,
fruit all flesh shall share together.

We gather here today to plant a new tomorrow,
watering these tender vines with waters from
the Jordan River mingled with waters from the United Nations,
in this sacred place – a garden of reconciliation and transformation.

We gather here today to plant a new tomorrow
asking the blessing of all that is holy
on our planting and pledging
our lives to be a holy planting.

We will go forth from here today
as many who are one,
who have planted together a new tomorrow
and pledged together to be a new tomorrow –

human gardens of reconciliation and transformation,
bearing the fruit of peace, justice and healing,
fruit all flesh shall share together,
in the name of all that is holy.

So may it be.

Filled With Amazement

Why not admit it –
sixty-three years on Earth
yet still an infant
filled with amazement
with so much left to learn!

Gratitude

O ver the decades, wherever I have found myself in the world, I have been blessed with inspired and inspiring companions, sharing the sacred and serving the world, on my pilgrim journey ever deeper into the heart of the Beloved.

To the Beloved and to all my companions, living in this world or on the other side of the veil – Thank you.

About the Author

C harles P. Gibbs is an internationally-respected spiritual leader, interfaith activist, speaker, and writer who has committed his life to serving the world through interreligious and intercultural engagement.

An Episcopal priest, he served for seventeen years as the founding executive director of the United Religions Initiative (www.uri.org), a global network of people from diverse religious and spiritual traditions united in service to the Earth community. He recently became senior partner and poet-in-residence for Catalyst for Peace (www.CatalystForPeace.org).

A prolific writer, Gibbs's published works include coauthoring *Birth of a Global Community*; contributing a chapter to *Interfaith Dialogue and Peacebuilding*; "Opening the Dream: Beyond the Limits of Otherness," an essay publishd in

Deepening the American Dream. For more information, visit www.revcharles-gibbs.net.

Charles cherishes and is inspired by his family. He is blessed with dear friends and colleagues of diverse faiths around the world. Mindful of the abundant blessings that come even through life's biggest challenges, he seeks to live each moment in gratitude. He currently resides in Kensington, MD.